WHAT DOES A FOREST RANGER DO?

DODD, MEAD & COMPANY · NEW YORK

WHAT DOES A FOREST RANGER DO?

by Wayne Hyde

Illustrated with photographs

TO MY MOTHER

ACKNOWLEDGMENTS

My sincere thanks and appreciation are extended to the following persons for their assistance and cooperation in the preparation of this book.

Dr. Matthew J. Brennan, Chief, Conservation Education Branch, U. S. Forest Service

Norman P. Weeden, Director of Cooperative Forest Fire Prevention, U. S. Forest Service

Leland J. Prater, Chief, U. S. Forest Service Photo Library — who took many of the photographs that appear in this book

Ann Hamilton, U. S. Forest Service Photo Library

WAYNE F. HYDE

Lookout tower

THE YOUNG forest ranger was the first to spot the thin column of smoke rising above the trees. As he sped toward the scene in his jeep he reported the fire on his two-way radio, giving its exact location. When he arrived there he saw it was a "surface fire"—the kind that burns dry leaves, twigs, grass and underbrush on the floor of the forest.

The ranger quickly began to spray the blaze with chemicals from a fire extinguisher, but the area was very dry and the fire was spreading faster than he could control it. If he could keep the blaze on the ground, keep it from climbing up into the pine trees, he had a good chance of stopping it—with the help of others who were now on the way in response to his radio call.

Suddenly flames licked at the trunk of a dry pine tree, ran up it and the tree "crowned" in an explosion of fire as its top burst into flame. Another and then another pine tree exploded into flaming torches and in a matter of seconds the ranger was completely surrounded by a wall of raging fire. He did not panic. He turned the nozzle of the fire extinguisher toward the ground

6

and sprayed the chemicals in a wide circle around him until the container was empty. Working as quickly as possible, he scraped a trench out of the soft ground with the shovel he had brought from the jeep. Then he lay down in the trench, raked the dirt from it over him and buried himself, making sure he could breathe. There he stayed until the fire passed over him. When it had moved on, he climbed out of the trench without so much as a singed eyebrow. The story is true. The forest ranger had been in similar situations before and he knew exactly what to do.

But fighting fires is only part of the ranger's job. Many people

Fire fighting is only part of a forest ranger's job

Heavily forested region

have only a vague idea of what a forest ranger does. They think of him as a man who stands in a lookout tower high above the ground, binoculars to his eyes, on the watch for forest fires. Actually, the man in the tower is usually not a forest ranger at all, but a member of a fire control organization who has been trained for such work by a forest ranger. He may be a young forester serving out his "apprenticeship," or training period. The "fire watch" job is only one of many he must do before he can become a full-fledged forest ranger. All forest rangers are foresters, but all foresters are not forest rangers.

Today's ranger supervises many men in an area that may cover thousands and thousands of acres. It is an enormous job. He must know how to build roads, survey forest areas, determine the extent of trees in a certain area and how fast they grow—and millions of trees may be involved. He must know how to treat trees for diseases and how to control insects that kill

8

trees. He even knows how to safeguard forests against damage by wind and snow. He knows how to care for wildlife, how to control floods and erosion, conduct timber sales, and many other things. We can safely say that forest rangers of today are engineers, surveyors, scientists, wildlife experts, businessmen and outdoorsmen, all rolled into one.

However, it was not always this way. Back in the 1870's our government realized that this country needed men trained in forestry in order to protect our forests, but there was not one school of forestry on this side of the Atlantic Ocean then. It was not until 1897 that Dr. C. A. Schenck came to this country from Germany and began giving private instruction in forestry. Two years later Cornell University and Yale University both had forestry schools in operation. But by 1912 there were still only about five hundred men in this country with some knowledge of

Old-time foresters at work, 1904

this important work—and these men were responsible for managing some 664 million acres of timberland.

Those early-day forest rangers were rugged men who could ride a horse with the best in the West. They were cowboys, trappers and woodsmen who traveled on horseback, on foot, in canoes—any way they could get to where they had to go. They knew very little about scientific ways of treating diseased trees or controlling insects, but they knew how to live in the woods and how to survive under any conditions. Their main job was to guard against forest fires, report them, and put them out if possible. They also kept a sharp lookout for "poachers"—men who hunt game or catch fish illegally—and they protected timberland and grazing land against those who tried to cut down trees or herd livestock in those areas. Through the years the early-day rangers built up a reputation for hard work and loyalty that is still in evidence today.

Today there are about 18,000 qualified foresters and rangers in the United States, but there are still not enough. There is a great demand for them; the field is wide open for anyone who can qualify.

How does one become a forest ranger? First of all, one must have a real love for nature and the outdoors. Being fond of camping in the open and of hunting and fishing is not enough. The forester's life is far different than that of the sportsman who camps out for a few weeks on vacation. The ranger lives for days, weeks, even months in the woods. His hours are long and irregular and he may be away from his home most of the time.

10

Forest rangers of bygone days. Above, J. C. Wells. At right, "Uncle Jim" Owen as photographed in 1920.

The work is very hard and there are times when the ranger is completely exhausted. He may be dirty, wet and cold at the same time. Travel in the woods can be difficult. In many areas there are no roads, so the ranger must be able to get around as best he can. He may spend hours on snowshoes, in a canoe, on horseback or on skis.

11

Sometimes the work is dangerous. The forest ranger must be able to keep his head in an emergency. A Forest Service snow ranger in Colorado was working alone when he struck a rock hidden under the snow. He broke a leg—but let him tell it:

"I also broke my left ski," he says, "so I used it to make a splint for my leg, tying it on with my leather shoe laces. Then I stood up on the one ski, pushed off with the ski poles and made it all the way back to the lodge on one leg. It was about six miles, but fortunately it was downhill all the way."

Ranger on winter elk survey

So the forest ranger must be strong, level-headed, and intelligent. He must be able to get along for long periods of time all alone, and, more than that, he must *like* the sort of life he will have to live.

A four-year college course is now required to become a forester. The student will have basic work in science, engineering, and economics. After four years of successful study he is graduated with a Bachelor of Science degree. He can specialize in one of several studies, including fisheries and wildlife, forestry, lum-

Forestry students marking a white oak for cutting

ber and building materials merchandising, forest management, wood technology, and many other fields. In many forestry schools there is a summer camp that students attend following their second year of study. These camps usually average about ten weeks, and during this time students get firsthand knowledge of the work of the forester. These field trips are required of all forestry students specializing in forestry management and forestry-wildlife management.

The study of forestry is not easy, and the boy planning to make a career of it has to be of above-average intelligence, have a natural scientific curiosity, and be a keen student—especially in the sciences. He should be able to get along well with people and express himself well. Most forest rangers are called upon often to speak to conservation groups, visitors to their areas, and others.

Who hires a forest ranger? The greater percentage of them work for the United States Forest Service, an agency of the Department of Agriculture. Others are with the National Park Service and spend their time working in such places as Yellowstone National Park or any one of our country's other National Parks. Still other rangers are teachers in forestry schools, and some are in private industry with big lumber companies. There are forest rangers in every one of our fifty states and Puerto Rico.

Ranger giving lecture

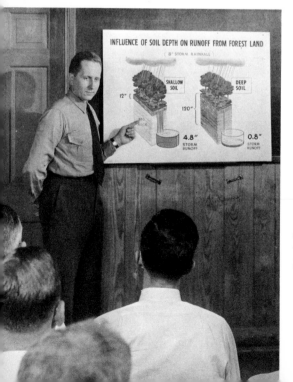

Some rangers—men with years of experience—are serving as forestry consultants and advisers in countries all over the world. For a qualified man in forestry there is always a good job waiting. In fact, there are more jobs than there are men to fill them.

Not every ranger does the same kind of work. One may specialize in forest management, another may be an expert on tree-killing diseases or insect control. Still others concentrate on wildlife management, or the important job of looking after grazing lands for livestock, or working against the causes of soil erosion.

The ranger who specializes in tree diseases and insect control has his hands full. Trees, like people, are subject to many diseases. Each year some twenty-eight and one-half million board feet of "sawtimber"—trees that can be sawed into lumber—are destroyed by insects or disease.

Making friends with a fawn

This is enough lumber to build two and one-half million five-room houses—enough for all the people living in New York City. Getting rid of forest insects and disease pests completely is impossible, but an effort is made to keep the damage done by them within limits. Forest rangers who specialize in this work supervise the spraying of their areas. When it is to be done by hand, hundreds of cans of "pesticides" are brought into the forest and unloaded at a "goop dump," as foresters call it.

The spray guns are filled and the "nozzle men" move through the infected areas in their protective masks and slickers, spraying the trees. This is done by hand only where small outbreaks of disease or insects are found—before they become epidemics. The pesticides used will not harm other living things.

15

Cans of pesticide at a "goop dump"

In larger areas, of course, the nozzle men cannot cover all the trees. Then machines, such as the mist-blower, are put to use. Or low-flying aircraft—both planes and helicopters—can be used effectively to cover great numbers of trees. They can spray hundreds of acres in far less time than any other machine yet devised.

The forest ranger's war against bugs and tree diseases never stops. The weapons used in the fight have proved effective over the years, but nature had a head start of thousands of years over man. Scientists are always trying to find new methods to combat these plagues of our forests.

16

Above, "nozzle man" in protective gear.
At left, plane spraying forested area.

A mist-blower in action spraying pines

Above, felling a "trap tree." At right, "ghost forest" caused by beetles that destroyed the trees.

Where it is possible, infested trees are cut down for lumber. If this cannot be done, the trees are felled and the insects in them destroyed. Foresters sometimes cut down a large tree that has not been infested. This is fresh food for the bugs—particularly bark beetles. The uninfested tree is called a "trap tree," and it is brought down because the beetles prefer a downed tree to one that is standing. Once the trap tree has been infested by the insects, it is sprayed. Then it may be cut up and used for lumber.

A forest epidemic can destroy thousands of trees, leaving them without foliage, stopping their growth. The entire area becomes a "ghost forest" of dead trees, a sad sight to see.

18

The forest ranger in charge of timber management for his district supervises all phases of lumbering. He determines which trees are ready for harvest, according to a management plan which shows where and how much timber will be cut each year. Rangers have to develop the growth of a timber area, so they make sure that the number of trees cut down is not larger than the number of those still growing. That is why you will see "staggered settings" of forest land in timber areas.

The cutting operation starts with a "timber cruise," to decide exactly what should be cut and what should be left. A map is made of the area showing the various types of timber, roads, trails and drainages. Then two-man cruise teams work through the forest using a compass and a "Biltmore stick." The Biltmore stick—named after the town of Biltmore, North Carolina—is used to estimate the diameter, height and number of board feet

Logging timber in "staggered settings" insures a continued crop

"Timber cruise" team using compass and Biltmore stick

of lumber in a tree. This gives the foresters a fairly accurate idea of how much lumber will come from the entire area. Since many trees are measured, the timber cruise may take some time.

Following the cruise team is a "marking team." Paint "guns" are filled with white paint and the markers spray a line of paint across the trunk of each tree to be cut. The base of the tree is

Close-up of Biltmore stick

Marking trees with a spray gun

marked, too, so that the ranger can check, even after the tree has been felled, to see that the right trees have been cut.

The Forest Service does not do any commercial logging, but sells its lumber to the highest bidder. The ranger and the private timber operator work closely together on all phases of the harvesting of Government timber. Then the lumberjacks move in. The lumber company "fallers"—the men who will cut the trees down—start their power saws and the forest rings with the sound of steel blades cutting through wood and the warning cries of "Timber!" as a big tree begins to fall.

"Faller" cutting a tree

The felled trees are then cut, or "bucked," into logs of the right length for hauling, and then are dragged, or "skidded," to a loading area where they are put on trucks.

But the ranger's work is not yet finished. An assistant then "scales" each log—that is, measures its diameter. The measurement is recorded and shows the amount of usable wood. The private timber operator pays the Government for the usable wood determined by this measurement. The entire cutting operations on a timber sale may take months or even years, depending on the amount of timber sold. During the entire operation the forest ranger supervises all phases to insure that the forest will not be damaged during lumbering and that a new young forest will soon replace the old. Money received from the sale of timber from the National Forests goes to the U. S. Treasury. Twenty-five per cent of this money goes to the county in which the forest is located, to be used for roads and schools.

22

Above, close-up of "faller" at work

At right, "scaling" for measurement

At left, "bucking" logs

Ranger and cattle rancher discuss condition of grazing range

In the western part of this country thousands of families depend upon Government-owned grazing land to feed their cattle and sheep. A permit from the Government is necessary in order to use the land. Ranchers pay a fee and are assigned certain grazing areas.

The forest ranger takes care of this, and he also looks after the range. It is his responsibility to see that there is enough forage, or food, for livestock, year after year—not only for cattle and sheep, but for big game animals which also use the ranges. He must make sure that there is enough grass and other forage plants left over to protect the land against floods and erosion—the wearing away of land by water or weather conditions.

The ranger keeps a constant check on the land in his district, talking with ranchers, riding the range with them. By carefully planned grazing, they can keep the land in good condition. The

Rancher and ranger counting sheep

number of animals in a certain area and the time they are allowed to graze there are carefully controlled. From time to time, livestock is moved from one range to another. And when the rancher moves his livestock, the forest ranger goes along. Each time a move is made, the stock is counted and recorded.

Sheep being moved to summer range

Soil moisture sampling

Sheep eat grass right down to the roots, and if they are not moved, they soon "eat the life out of the grass." Baked under a hot sun, the short grass will wither and die. A heavy rain or a snow melt will then wash it away and the topsoil beneath it. Rangers take samplings of the soil, not only in grazing lands but in many sections of their districts, to see how much moisture there is in the ground. They can then determine if the land will need water development.

At times soil becomes so eroded that grass and other small plants will not grow in it. Young trees are sometimes planted in these sections, with careful attention given to the place-ment of each so it will do the most good in helping to renew the soil.

26

Water flowing through a national forest is the forest's most valuable resource. That is why forest rangers pay constant attention to the water needs of their districts. Streams must be clean and the water supply must be kept plentiful. The land must be protected against erosion from water, but it must have adequate irrigation too.

Forest rangers set up and maintain snow evaporation stations to give an accurate measurement of moisture from melting snow. The instruments at these stations show the amount of snowfall in a certain area. They also show how much snow has melted in a twenty-four hour period when the spring thaw comes. By making regular checks at these stations, rangers can tell how much water runoff to expect.

Snow evaporation station where moisture from melting snow is measured

If you have ever visited one of our National Forests or Parks you will have noticed that there are always good campsites with benches, tables, fireplaces and safe drinking water. Forest rangers are responsible for these sites, and it is a never-ending job. Each year more and more people visit these campsites and thoughtless persons destroy or damage equipment, or leave litter behind after camping. Foresters spend much of their time keeping the Parks in good shape.

Forest rangers are also responsible for the safety of visitors to their areas. The Arapaho National Forest in Colorado is a favorite recreation spot for skiers and other winter sports enthusiasts. Here the snow rangers are at work. These men are expert skiers, among the best in the world. They are equally at home on snowshoes, dog sleds, or any other kind of transportation used in deep snow.

In winter months there is a great deal of snow in the Arapaho, and while snow can be a lot of fun, it can be dangerous too. The snow rangers make it as safe as they possibly can. They watch the snowfall, measure it, determine whether it is likely to stay on the hills and mountains. If there is danger of a possible snowslide, a ranger will post a warning sign: DANGER—AVALANCHE AREA—KEEP OUT.

Warning sign posted by ranger

Bangalore torpedoes being set in place

Sometimes small avalanches are started deliberately by the snow rangers—but only when no one is around—to bring the snow down and thus eliminate the danger of a large avalanche or snowslide. Avalanches are unpredictable and dangerous. Simply shouting or a turn on skis can start one and, without warning, tons of snow will cascade down a hillside or mountainside, carrying along everything in the path, burying houses, vehicles—and people.

The snow ranger knows how to tell when snow is building up to the danger point and what to do about it. He may place "bangalore torpedoes" along the top of a snow ridge to blast away an avalanche before it reaches a dangerous size. These are pieces of metal tubing filled with explosives and set off by either a time fuse or by electrical contact from a detonator.

Above, 105 mm. recoilless rifle on mount. At right, snow ranger sights 75 mm. rifle.

During World War II they were used to blast paths through barbed wire entanglements or through mine fields.

Avalanche control rangers are on duty in many states. In the Wasatch National Forest in Utah, another winter sports area, rangers use a 105-millimeter recoilless rifle as an "avalanche buster." The gun, the first of its kind in the United States, is mounted on a permanent installation and revolves in a complete circle, making it possible to fire in any direction.

The ski patrol rangers in Tahoe National Forest in California use a similar weapon, a 75-millimeter recoilless rifle. Less powerful than the 105, this smaller rifle is portable and can be carried where it is needed. In another California ski area rangers have adapted a device widely used by big-league baseball teams. Called an "Avalauncher," it is a converted gas-operated baseball

"Busted" avalanche in motion six seconds after shell exploded

launcher which will fire a two-pound explosive charge up to a distance of a quarter-mile. It is less expensive to use than either the 75 mm. or 105 mm. guns, and the snow rangers report that it "shoots down" avalanches very effectively.

Once an avalanche is "busted," the huge snow slabs come hurtling down the hill or mountainside. Sometimes there is a roar of sound as the tons of snow sweep downward, and one only has to see an avalanche in action to realize the tremendous power of it, even though it is one that has been shot down before it is "full grown." Experts in judging the danger point in a possible avalanche, the snow rangers never let ridges build up to a degree where they can become real hazards.

Using "handitalkie" radio

Radio relay station

Snow control is only one of the ways in which forest rangers try to make this country's National Parks as safe as possible. Occasionally, however, someone does become ill or injured while in the woods. Suppose it is a forester or lumberjack working in a remote area where there are no roads. The ranger knows how to get help. Every lumbering operation has some form of communication. It may be a 12-pound "handitalkie" carried on the back of a man, and able to transmit, or to be heard, from five to thirty miles. The information is broadcast from the small transmitter, possibly picked up by one of several radio relay stations in the area where it can be sent out on a more powerful frequency.

Within a matter of minutes help can be on the way. It might be in the form of one of the Forest Service patrol planes which can land on and take off from the

Above, Forest Service patrol plane

At right, helicopter pilot unstraps stretcher carrying injured man

ground, water, or snow. During the fire danger season these patrol planes are in the sky every day, their pilots on the alert for fires or smoke. They have also acted as flying ambulances during emergencies.

But it is the small helicopter which has proved to be the most useful vehicle to the forest ranger. Able to get into and out of places no plane can go—and where sometimes even a jeep cannot go—the little "eggbeater," especially equipped to carry two patients in stretchers, has flown injured men from deep in the woods directly to hospitals. It has other uses, too, in spotting fires from the air, dropping supplies, searching for persons lost in the woods, surveying forest lands from the air, tree spraying, putting fire fighters into a fire area and picking them up again.

Rescue of baby fawn only ten hours old from dense forest thicket

The forest ranger who specializes in wildlife management has a genuine liking for all animals, large and small, and he proves this in his daily work. The shade of very dense forests keeps food for animals from growing on the ground among the trees. The ranger knows this and one of his jobs is to provide food for wildlife, so he has clearings cut in dense timber land so that sunlight can reach the ground. In these clearings he may plant small trees and other plants for wildlife food. The animals seem to like these places, seem to know that they can find plenty of food in them. Deer, particularly, are found often in the food clearings.

When the timber crop is harvested, the ranger tries to leave

At right, black bear cub on a tree
near a campsite

A white-tailed deer seen in a forest clearing

hollow trees standing because raccoons and other small animals use them for dens. Nut-bearing trees are left for the animals that eat this kind of food. Knowing that small animals need cover and concealment from their natural enemies, the ranger plants shrubs at the edge of the food clearings. Thus, a small animal can get out of sight quickly when a larger one approaches. Pine trees, which keep their needles, are planted among oaks, maples and other hardwoods because they make good winter cover when the leaves have fallen. This gives wildlife protection from heavy snows.

The forest ranger works closely with men of the state fish and game departments to provide better hunting and fishing for those who like these outdoor sports. Together, the ranger and the game warden make surveys to determine the number of deer, bear, elk or other wildlife in a certain area. The information is made public so that hunters and fishermen will know what places have game for hunting and fish for catching.

But wildlife needs protection from too much hunting and fishing also. Each state has its own laws limiting the number of fish and animals that can be taken, and establishing only certain seasons for sportsmen to hunt and fish. The game wardens enforce these laws, but the forest rangers help them as much as possible. Unfortunately, there are some hunters who think nothing of killing a female animal even when she has her young with her. Rangers sometimes find these newly-born animals and take care of them until they are old enough to take care of themselves. Then they are released.

Wildlife rangers can tell some interesting stories. There was the ranger who saw a large deer trapped between two trees, unable to free herself. He found he could not bend the trees far enough to release her, but if he left her there she would probably die or be killed by wolves or a mountain lion. There was only one thing to do. He would sacrifice one of the trees to save the deer. Using a saw, he cut the tree down while the big doe lay there peacefully. "I thought she might be hurt," the ranger says, "so I tried to help her up. She made it to her feet all right. But did she thank me for freeing her? No, she kicked me and ran off!"

That ranger was more fortunate than the one who tangled with a mother bear, however. He was watching her and her cub

Doe trapped by trees was rescued by forest ranger

when the mother bear scented him. She quickly cuffed her cub into the underbrush, then turned and charged the ranger. This is unusual, according to the ranger, because most bears will not attack unless molested. But a mother with a young cub is unpredictable. The ranger headed toward a nearby stream with mama right after him. She clawed at him and severely scratched his leg before he dived headfirst into the stream and swam underwater for some distance. When he surfaced, the bear and her cub were just disappearing into the woods.

It is not unusual in some of the National Parks to see bears on the roads, stopping cars and begging for food. Rangers warn visitors to keep their car windows closed and not to feed the bears. They may look friendly but they are still wild animals.

Rangers will tell you that watching wildlife in its natural surroundings is an education in itself. In the 180 million acres

Bear cubs look friendly, but they are still wild animals

Ranger shows youngsters how the "Kortick Tool," a combined rake and hoe, is used to clear a line around a fire

of our National Forests live about three and one-third million big game animals, plus untold numbers of smaller animals and birds. The work of the forest ranger helps both the forest and the animals, which are dependent on one another. Plants and animals cannot live without water. Streams and lakes dry up when the plant cover is not heavy enough to preserve rainfall and snow. Some trees and plants depend upon certain animals for distribution of their seeds, and some animals depend upon certain plants for their food. One could not get along without the other. By improving the forest, the ranger is also making sure that wildlife is preserved.

39

A "surface fire" rages through a forest

Almost one-third of the United States is forest land—approximately 664 million acres of it. Each year thousands of fires burn and scar some 30 million of those acres. The sawtimber that goes up in flames each year is enough to build 86,000 five-room homes. The major cause of these fires is human carelessness or negligence.

Fire control is one of the jobs of every forest ranger, no matter whether he is a wildlife expert, a timber management ranger, or an insect and tree-disease specialist. When fire breaks out in a forest all other work stops and every man available joins in fighting the blaze. It may go on for hours, days, even weeks, and a forest ranger—the "fire boss"—directs the fire fighting.

Foresters say, "The best way to stop a fire is never to let it start." The ranger keeps up with the latest weather conditions at all times, especially in the late summer and early autumn when the danger of fires is greater because of dry weather. He makes daily checks at various points in the forest and records information from special instruments placed in these locations to measure the dryness of the air.

The ranger is also responsible for a fire control organization. He helps in the training of such a group, decides where it will be placed, what kind of equipment it will have, and supervises every aspect of his fire control unit.

Ranger recording fire danger weather data

Locating a fire in its early stages is very important in the successful control of the fire. The Forest Service has a network of permanently established lookout stations on mountain peaks and other high ground. All of them are equipped with telephones, two-way radio receivers and transmitters, and other communications, and the lookout men must know how to use this equipment and even repair it if necessary.

Checking for forest fires

In seasons when fire danger is high there are also "secondary lookouts" in other towers equipped with telephones. There are also men on foot or horseback on constant fire patrol, and Forest Service patrol planes in the skies to spot fires from the air.

Lookout on duty telephones information about fire

42

Lookout towers are now equipped with "fire finders" that give the towerman an accurate location when he spots a "smoke." One type in use is mounted on a map table which is placed so that the map directions agree with the compass directions on the ground. By sighting through the two arms of the fire finder —much as you might aim a rifle with a telescopic sight—the lookout man can record the exact distance from his tower to the fire and the azimuth, or compass point, of the fire. With these measurements and other landmarks he can telephone the location of the smoke to the district ranger or to a central fire dispatcher. As he talks on the phone, he will keep an eye on the fire location and report any new developments if they occur.

Towerman sights through fire finder to spot location of a "smoke"

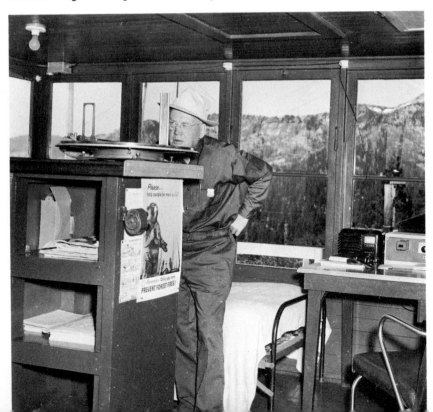

Suppression crew in action

The dispatcher or district ranger may receive other readings on the fire from other lookout stations. He then quickly plots the azimuth readings on his own map. When he has the information concerning location, size and spread of the fire, and the type of fuel or material that is burning, he sends out a "suppression crew." With the information from the dispatcher, they know what to do. "Suppression crew," of course, is another name for fire fighters. A small fire can usually be put out by one to five men. Larger fires may require as many as a thousand men.

"Surface fires"—those that burn along the ground—are sometimes easy to control, but they kill seedlings and small trees. And every small forest fire can become a big one in a matter of seconds. If the area is dry and a high wind comes up suddenly, the small fire may leap upward to the treetops. In pine forests this is a constant danger because pines, unlike broad-leaved trees, will burn fiercely. Fires that sweep through the tops of trees are called "crown fires" and are the most dangerous. Dry pines literally explode when flames reach them, scattering sparks and blazing embers to other parts of the forest and starting new fires.

A raging forest fire is a terrifying sight. It roars through the trees faster than a man can run—faster than a *deer* can run—burning everything in its path.

A "crown fire" in treetops

The result is another kind of "ghost forest"—blackened remains of trees, all grass and vegetation gone, sometimes homes and other buildings burned to the ground. Forest fires kill many animals and birds. Wood ashes washed into a stream after a fire can kill fish, and vegetation burned along the banks of streams may cause water temperature to rise, making the stream unfit for fish.

Nine-tenths of all forest fires are caused by humans. Smokers alone have been responsible for 19 per cent of all fires each year. A carelessly tossed cigarette, a match that has not been completely put out can start a small fire that can rapidly become a big one. Lightning striking a dry forest can also start a blaze, but lightning storms cause only 4 per cent of forest fires each year.

Burned out forest caused by a careless hunter's cooking fire

Lightning striking trees

Forest rangers supervise two methods of fire fighting—the "direct" and "indirect" attacks. Direct attack, the work directly on the burning edge of the fire, can be used only on a slow-burning blaze where the heat is not too great. Suppression crews do this by raking or sweeping burning embers back into the fire, beating out flames with wet sacks, brooms, even green branches, or by using water.

Indirect attack means working at some distance from the blaze. Men construct "firelines" by scraping away all vegetation and fuel for the fire right down to the bare earth. This can be done with a bulldozer at times, and the fireline is varied in width, depending upon the size of the fire, how fast it is spreading, and the condition of the soil. Crewmen with hand tools follow the bulldozer to clear away anything the "dozer" blade

47

"Direct attack" on edge of fire

has missed, and there is usually a tanker truck nearby with a water hose. Indirect attack has to be some distance from the fire to allow the men time enough to get the fireline built before the blaze reaches them. If the fireline is wide enough, the fire will stop there; it has nothing more to feed on then.

A "backfire" is another way of stopping an advancing blaze, but it takes an expert to set one. The idea is to start the backfire at a natural barrier, such as a road, stream, or railroad—a barrier that the oncoming flames cannot jump. The backfire is set along this line and allowed to burn back to the main fire, thus removing the combustible fuel in front of the main fire. But a backfire can "backfire" on the person setting it if he is not entirely familiar with its uses, and forest rangers select only the fire fighters who have had a great deal of experience in this work for this job.

You will recall the young ranger who buried himself in the ground to escape a forest fire that surrounded him. With the new portable shelter developed by the Forest Service this may no longer be necessary. Made of fireproof aluminized cloth, the shelter folds up to the size of a rolled newspaper and can be attached to a man's belt. If trapped by flames, the fire fighter

Bulldozer clearing a fireline

Portable fire shelter used by fire fighters

squats down on the ground, pulls the shelter over him, and waits it out. Tests have shown that while temperatures outside the shelter were 600 degrees Fahrenheit, they were only 130 degrees inside. Uncomfortably warm, perhaps, but the shelter is a probable life-saver.

50

Attack from the air on forest fires is another method of fighting them. As early as 1919, the Forest Service was experimenting with the use of airplanes for fire detection. Today there are many different ways to fight fire from the air. One is the use of "smokejumpers"—parachuting fire fighters especially trained for their hazardous work.

Many of these young men are forestry students. Wearing heavily padded suits, helmets and face masks to guard them against landings in trees or other rough terrain, they jump in teams of at least two, landing as close to the fire as possible. They carry fire-fighting tools with them—more may be dropped to them later—and they go to work as soon as they are out of their parachutes. It might take hours to get to a fire by traveling on the ground in some remote areas, but it takes only minutes to reach the fire by parachute. Smokejumping is dangerous, but these men have made nearly 13,000 jumps since 1940 with very few serious injuries.

Smokejumpers parachuting to scene of fire

At left, smokejumper removes fire fighting tools from parachute pack

At right, "helijumper" in special protective gear is ready to jump

Then there are the "helijumpers"—the men who come in by helicopter. They, too, wear the protective clothing worn by smokejumpers because, although a helicopter can get close to the ground, heavy brush may prevent it from landing. The helijumper leaps from the 'copter at a height of from five to ten feet from the ground, gets out of his protective gear and goes to work.

Helijumping is used in areas where it is too dangerous to parachute, where there are jagged rocks or spiny plants, or where a fire is spreading too fast. Both smokejumpers and helijumpers have "pinned" and held small fires under control on many occasions—fires that might have become big ones. This is their chief purpose. They stay until the fire is "dead out," as they call it, or until a fire crew arrives. Then they may be picked up by a helicopter or they may have to walk out to a place where a truck or jeep will be waiting for them.

The Forest Service uses the small helicopter for many pur-

Helicopters speed up fire fighting

poses. On a big fire, the forest ranger acting as fire boss may be up in a helicopter over the area. From there he can see things that his ground crews cannot, and can direct the men on the ground by radio. This has proved very effective in controlling forest fires.

If you have ever tugged a garden hose around your yard you know what effort it takes. That will give you some idea of what a difficult job it is to drag thousands of feet of heavy fire hose up steep rocky slopes. Until recently, fire fighters did this by hand. Now helicopters have joined the hose-laying team. The hose is folded into a tray mounted under the 'copter. The helicopter takes off, the pilot pushes a button and a coiled length of hose is released. The weight of the coil pulls the rest of the hose

Packing fire hose into a helicopter tray

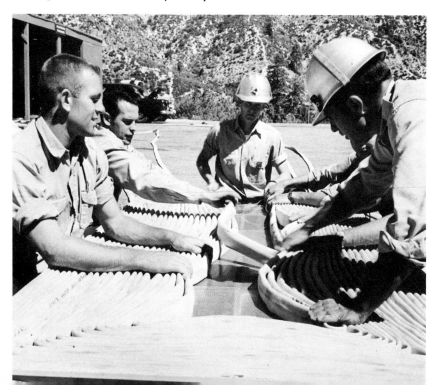

Laying fire hose from a helicopter

out of the tray as the 'copter flies slowly forward. The nozzle end of the hose is the last to fall. If more hose lengths are needed the helicopter returns to a point where pre-packed hose trays replace the empty ones. On one fire, twenty sections of hose totaling 10,000 feet were laid in this manner. Ground crews easily connected the separate sections.

Helicopter hose-laying works well. In a test demonstration it took eight ground crewmen thirty minutes to lay 1,500 feet of hose up a 70 per cent slope. A helicopter did the same job in only fifty-three seconds.

The little "whirlybirds" also serve as "helitankers," dropping water or chemical fire retardant on small fires and lightning-struck trees. A pyramid-shaped fabric bag containing thirty-five gallons of liquid is suspended under the helicopter. On the bottom of the bag is a long neck that it drawn up through the bag and fastened to a tripping mechanism. As the 'copter hovers directly over the fire, the pilot pushes a button releasing the neck of the bag, and the water or chemical is dropped onto the fire.

Thirty-five gallons of liquid dropped in this way can cover an area 10 to 15 feet wide and 50 to 75 feet long. When empty, the bag is so light and compact that it can be carried in a briefcase. Spare bags are filled at loading spots near the fire and are quickly and easily exchanged for the empty ones, enabling the heli-tankers to drop water or retardants on fires every few minutes. During one forest fire, 77 helitanker drops were made, releasing more than 2,600 gallons with pinpoint accuracy, knocking the flames out of the trees and cooling the fire area enough to allow ground crews to come in and get the fire under control.

Although airplanes are not as maneuverable as helicopters, they can carry larger amounts of water or fire retardant, and the Forest Service has found them quite effective in providing close aerial support for ground crews. During a bad fire that burned over 3,500 acres, ground crews fighting the blaze in a valley were threatened by spreading flames on a ridge above them. The fire boss ranger ordered a "borate" drop. Borate is a chemical mixture that penetrates foliage better than water and re-

"Helitankers" are used to drop chemicals on a fire. Thirty-five gallons of liquid are released at the push of a button.

tards fire for a longer period of time. Three planes, two of them Navy Torpedo Bombers, or TBM's, dropped one load each on the ridge fire, totaling 2,100 gallons. The blaze was completely extinguished.

The TBM, no longer in use by the U. S. Navy, is widely used by the Forest Service. These air tankers can knock out small ground fires and cool down hot spots so that men can enter an area and work safely. They can lay a fire-retardant line in ad-

Torpedo Bomber releasing chemical on a fire

vance of a fire, thus enabling ground crews to build a fireline, and they can fireproof areas in very dry fire seasons before a fire has a chance to break out. They cannot make safe drops in high winds, however, nor can they make drops in the bottoms of steep canyons or other places where there is not room enough for them to maneuver. And they cannot work at night. So, while they can help ground crews, they cannot replace them. The mop-up operations in any forest fire must still be done by the men on the ground. But the Forest Service's air war against fires is improving each year. New fire retardants are being developed that are less expensive than the ones now in use. And in this age of rocketry, some thought is being given to what a guided missile full of fire retardant could do, especially in high winds and where visibility is very poor.

One of the newest training aids for ground fire fighters is the Fire Control Simulator. Twelve trainees sit at four tables with communication equipment in front of them. They face an 8 by 12-foot screen on which an aerial view of a forest fire is projected. One trainee acts as the fire boss. In a separate booth sit three members of the training staff—an audio-visual operator, a "role player" and an umpire. The umpire gives the trainees simulated weather conditions, types of fuel in the path of the fire, and other information. Then the role player, acting as one of the ground crew, phones a trainee with a problem. He may say that there are campers in the fire area who have to be located and taken out. By using the communication equipment, the trainee must give the order that he feels will bring the best results. He may call a helicopter, water trucks, or more ground crew men onto the scene.

Trainees watching Fire Control Simulator screen

Fire Control Simulator booth and trainees

Meanwhile, by the use of three different projectors and two tape recorders, the audio-visual operator is supplying sound effects and projecting fire and smoke on the screen. The fire is represented by a red line that can be moved into any position on the screen. As the fire boss trainee gives his commands, the screen shows the results. The umpire judges how well the trainees are doing in controlling the fire. The entire unit can be used indoors or outdoors, and can be moved to various training locations on a specially designed automobile trailer. It provides good experience in learning how to fight forest fires without the loss of timber.

Smokey as a cub with fire prevention sign

Most of you have seen the "Smokey Bear" forest fire prevention posters. Perhaps many of you are Junior Forest Rangers, for there are about four million of them in the United States today. The Smokey program was started in 1945 especially to get boys and girls interested in forest fire prevention, and the result has been excellent. It has meant fewer forest fires in this country simply because the Junior Forest Rangers know how to prevent them from starting.

Real forest rangers at times give instruction to the Junior Forest Rangers, and keep them informed as to the latest fire fighting procedures. Smokey Bear Clubs are now in every one of our fifty states and also in Puerto Rico.

Smokey is a real bear, not just a drawing on a poster. His story starts in the Lincoln National Forest in New Mexico. It was a very dry day in May of 1942 when someone was careless with a match, a cigarette, or a campfire.

61

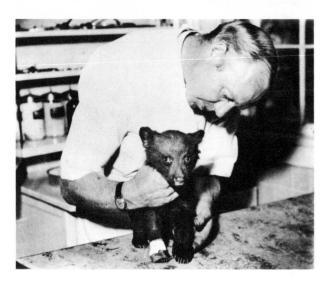

The real Smokey being treated
for burns by a veterinarian

No one knows just how the fire started, but it spread quickly. Hundreds of men battled the raging blaze, and twenty-four of them nearly lost their lives when a strong wind swept the flames toward them. They ran to a rock slide and lay face down, covering their faces with wet handkerchiefs while the fire passed over them. When the smoke and flame finally cleared, the only living thing those men saw was a badly burned and badly frightened little bear cub clinging to a blackened tree. How he survived the terrible fire is not known.

Carefully the men lifted him off the tree and took him to a forest ranger station. Rangers, veterinarians and men from the

Full grown Smokey at the
zoo in Washington, D. C.

New Mexico Game and Fish Department took care of the little cub's wounds and burns. The kind treatment paid off and the cub got better each day. Because they had found him in the smoke the rangers named him Smokey, and the name stuck.

Today Smokey is a full grown black bear and lives in the National Zoological Park in Washington, D. C., where thousands of visitors come to see him each year.

He has become a national symbol in preventing forest fires, and his Junior Forest Rangers have helped tremendously in cutting down the number of forest fires and the damage caused by them. Under the direction of a former forest ranger, the Forest Service has a full-time staff in Washington just to take care of the thousands of post cards and letters that come in each week from children who want to become Junior Forest Rangers. There is no charge for joining this fast-growing and important organization; it is absolutely free. You may join simply by writing to: Smokey Bear Headquarters, Washington 25, D. C.

Forest rangers do not lead an easy life, but they are among the most dedicated men in this country. Because they are helping to guard and improve our National Forests, they are making an important and necessary contribution to the security and strength of our country.

They are truly in your service.

WHAT TO DO WHEN LOST IN THE WOODS

Forest rangers say it is better to carry a clear head on your shoulders than a big pack on your back. But when going alone into the forest it is well to go prepared to get lost. If this should happen to you, the following helpful rules are worth remembering:

1. Stop, sit down, and try to figure out where you are. Use your head, not your legs.

2. If caught by night, fog, or a storm, stop at once and get into a sheltered spot—a ledge, a large boulder, or a fallen tree. Clear a space of ground, and build a fire. If you have no blanket for warmth, you can build your fire in a deep hole, using plenty of dry wood. Make sure it is in a safe place. When the fire burns down to hot coals—about six inches of them—cover it with six inches of earth, and sleep on the warmed earth. If you cannot build a fire, even leaves or branches will offer some shelter.

3. Don't wander around. Travel only downhill.

4. If injured or ill, choose a clear spot and make a signal smoke. Green leaves on a small fire make a lot of smoke.

5. Don't yell, don't run, don't worry and, above all, DON'T QUIT. If you are lost, someone will be looking for you.